Enjoy

Ruth O'Lill

Songs to Sisters

Songs to Sisters

A Celebration of Being Woman

Ruth O'Lill and Lynn Olcott

J. Dunn & Company, Publishers   Virginia Beach   Virginia

J. Dunn & Company, Publishers
P.O. Box 1479
Virginia Beach, VA 23451

If you are unable to order this book from your local bookseller, you may order directly from the publisher. Quantity discounts are available.

O'Lill, Ruth, 1948-
    Songs to sisters : a celebration of being woman / by Ruth O'Lill and Lynn Olcott.
        p.   cm.
    ISBN 0-9659214-1-7
    1. Sisters—Poetry. 2. Women—Poetry   I. Olcott, Lynn
    II. Title.
    PS3565.L4518S66   1999
    811' .54—dc21
                                                                    99-20397
                                                                    CIP

ISBN 0-9659214-1-7

Cover painting by Pam Ogden

Pamela Martin Ogden works in a variety of media. Her work has been selected for numerous exhibitions and awards. She has commissioned work on both coasts. She is a native of Roanoke, Virginia, a graduate of Radford University, and a resident of Salem. Virginia. When not painting, she sails competitively with her husband, does long-distance bicycling, camps, hikes, canoes, and is involved in environmental issues through serving on boards or sitting in front of bulldozers.

Cover design by John Comerford and Kim Cohen
Book design by Kim Cohen

To my sister
and
all our sisters –
and
brothers –
along the way.

Songs to Sisters

Table of Contents

Acknowledgments

There are many women, and a few men, who have supported us on the long journey that has become this book.

An enduring thank-you to Clare Charlie, Karen Ross Doxtater, Claire Grant, Karel Horak, Syd Judson, Colleen Keane, Cheryl Leban, Susan Lewis, Pat MacMaster, Ira Nix, Mary Babcock Rock, Harvey and Jeannie Steinberg, Dee Dee Wendland, Valerie Wilkinson, and Madeline Chernow Witter. A special thank-you to Bonnie Begay who typed the very first draft 20 years ago.

To the publisher and editor, Joe Dunn, who saw a larger message in our very private words. This would not be a book without his vision of our work and his commitment to us to share our story in print.

To our mother, Ruth Jones Olcott, who we believe is never far away.

To our father, Dr. William Olcott, a masterful word-smith, who is still encouraging us to take risks, to speak from our hearts, and to eat our vegetables.

For always believing in our words, we especially want to thank Dr. Marion Potts.

To our remarkable children, bless them, for they have made us better women. By order of age they are: William Thomas Lill Jr., Chester Jones Lill, Bonnie Lynn Lill Yannotti, Damien Kee Hoffman-Olcott, and Ande Dylan Olcott.

And to our grandchildren, Joslyn Olivia Yannotti and Fletcher Cleveland Lill, who have made us feel immortal.

Introduction

Songs to Sisters is written by two sisters who share the same parents, the same eyes, the same cheekbones, and the same spirit.

In our late teens, life launched the two of us in dramatically different directions, but we kept our bond strong through the mail. We didn't write letters; letters seemed too breezy and newsy. We were drawn instead to the intimacy of poetry as a way to share our joys and our fearful times. Through the years, our closeness and our poetry grew as we explored and shared the fullness of the female experience.

The words came naturally to our fingers, perhaps more through our hearts than our heads, as a meaningful way to share our lives with each other. "The sky is blue, the grass is green" just didn't seem enough — not when you want someone you love to see and to feel the path you are walking. We each assumed that all sisters innately share deeply and descriptively with each other.

The poems also came from the times we missed each other most — not at our crowded weddings, but when we were each alone folding laundry or curling our hair. They came from the longing for a really good friend to be close by.

At the time we didn't pay much attention to how we communicated. We simply knew that living so far apart, we needed the special kind of closeness experienced by other sisters and women. Looking back, it seems that the greater the miles, the more intimate our messages.

We began our correspondence in the late 1960s. Standing over our mother's grave, we hugged each other goodbye and went separate ways from our small-town home in Upstate New York - never to return.

Lynn developed a mobile and rustic life, living in grass huts in Africa and trailers on Indian reservations in the West. She saved the poems she received in a small sewing box tucked beneath a small hand-hewn bench. Both accompanied her when she moved to new cultures and new lands.

Ruth went to the middle-class suburbs with car pools, soccer games, diapers, and dinner parties. She saved her sister's words in a dresser drawer with potpourri to pull out and reread in the too long, too hectic, too predictable times.

We didn't plan to save our letters. But not being arm-in-arm for lunches, birthdays, weddings, births, or lab tests, our poems began to fashion a different kind of memory. A memory that we could hold.

Our letters were precious, read in quiet corners of our days or nights and tucked away as proof that we had each other always — no matter what. This book is evidence that we have been steadfast creative partners, believing in each other as sisters, daughters, writers, mothers, and people.

Through the years, we have offered some of these words as insights to a few close friends. A Sioux woman who had fallen in love with and married a Navajo man while both lived at a Bureau of Indian Affairs boarding school. She found our letters beautiful, woman-based, and close to her heart as she struggled with her "mixed tribe" marriage. A neighbor, Ivy, with her British outlook and sparkling house found our letters beyond judgment. She could come out from behind her properness and relax with our words. A confident young stepdaughter-in-law who reigns over her life in Cleveland saw that a balance is possible between female fluff and female force.

Our poems continue today, now about our growing children, our grandchildren, our recoveries from divorce, our new lives and careers, and our parallel paths as adult women.

The words in this volume, however, are no longer the private conversations of two blood sisters. These words, these thoughts, these feelings also belong to you – to every woman who is traveling her own odyssey. Our correspondence, as personal as loving sisters and as universal as womanhood, chronicles the journeys of women through loves, losses, stretch-marks, and successes. It acknowledges that each woman's journey has its own pitstops and palaces along the way.

Songs to Sisters will evoke different thoughts for different readers. Its theme, however, clearly reflects the sometimes remarkable, sometimes grudging steps our society has taken to lift women from the long list of supporting players and to give us a starring role with men in this fascinating drama called life.

This book is a tribute to where you are on your own path. If you sense our hard-earned wisdom, you must be proud of your own. If you barely remember your past pain; you, too, have healed.

We invite you to become our sister. Travel with us through these pages on our journey and meet our children, our parents, our lovers, our friends. They are yours, too.

Share with us our fears and lessons. They are yours, too.

Celebrate with us, dear reader, for there is a part of you somewhere in every line.

Siamese Sisters

Siamese sisters,
time zones apart,
joined at the laughlines,
joined at the heart.

Blood
Sisters

Blood Sisters

Our parents met at what would become our future high school. Dad was the pensive history teacher and broad-shouldered, young football coach. Mom was the new home economics teacher with huge Welsh eyes – dark, wide, and wet; eyes that the two of us inherited. Our family moved several times before finally settling in Cortland, a small college town amid the huge green hills and deep iron-rich lakes of Upstate New York.

Lynn's side of the shared bedroom was always quiet and clean. There was a calm order to her belongings. Ruthy's was a cauldron of clothes, sneakers, stuffed animals, and papers.

Lynn, the older by two years, was the daughter who could sit still and discuss homework and current events at the table. Ruthy, named for her mother, was funny, athletic, and much like a puppy – if they played with her enough, she wouldn't chew at the fabric of the family.

As young girls, we watched our parents go back to school - father for a Ph.D. and mother for a master's degree in health education. Dad became a professor at the local college. Mom stayed home and used her education to do volunteer work, substitute in high school and college classrooms, and teach us how to sew, cook, paint, and play. The house was full of books and craft projects.

Our family spent every summer camping. We felt closest during those sun-blessed camping days when we made cookies and cakes of sand on a wooden dock and decorated them with berries, flowers, feathers, and stones. Every teacher-length summer, the family homesteaded in the Adirondack Mountains, carefully picking our spot on a clover-shaped lake safely surrounded by platoons of long, lean white birch trees.

Together we four pitched and ditched our tents, made little stools out of chunks of fat fallen trees, and built a dock to launch our ancient, authentic Adirondack guideboat.

We learned to collect dry wood for our fires; we learned to roll and unroll our Mom-made, fur-lined sleeping bags; we learned to always keep our sister-shared canvas floor swept of sand and our canvas house zipped from bugs, to always cover our wood from the rain; and to always keep the lid tight on the cooler.

We started the crisp mornings dressed in layers and by midday had peeled down to our bathing suits. As the sun slowly withdrew, we added flannels and wools and, by nighttime, even stocking caps. We would be cozy for the evening fire and storytelling. Neighboring campers often drifted over with their lawn chairs to hear Dad recite long poems filled with lyrical words and cricket-chirping pauses.

Despite all the chores that come with camping, we experienced incredible freedom during those outdoor days and nights. We learned to take care of our own "stuff" while running through the woods, paddling a boat around the lake, hiking for fresh blueberries, and protecting our campsite from curious raccoons.

The rest of the year we sisters did not get along as well. The roles we played in school were different from in the woods. Expectations from our circle of friends, neighbors, teachers, and preachers weighed heavily on us during the school year. Those were the days when girls were expected to sit still, be quiet, and watch sports from the sidelines. Only one sister, Lynn, could comply.

Our family attended a little cobblestone Unitarian Universalist church in Cortland. Our faith and our family were the most liberal things about our young lives. Our Catholic friends couldn't understand our religion; they needed special permission from their priests to come with us to church. Only two families in our entire school district attended our church; the rest of our church youth group came from neighboring communities. We learned early about not belonging, and we learned as well about being proud of ourselves and proud of what we truly believed.

Within the warmth and safety of small-town life, our mother died a cold, silent death. Lynn was seventeen. Ruthy was fifteen. The two of us would not camp together again for twenty years. In those days no one discussed cancer, and we endured a suffocating silence. We were in our late teens when, motherless, our last stage of girlness was ended, and we began to keep our first and saddest family secret — cancer.

Our mother died when she was in her middle forties, younger than we are now. She had lived the dichotomy of a traditional, stay-at-home mom who was bright, strong, and independent and who always kept one high heel in the workaday world. She bequeathed to us a confidence in our ability to create — whether we were making sand cakes, prom dresses, doll houses, poems, or babies. But what we remember most was her telling us that every time she looked at the moon she saw the image of a beautiful woman instead of a man. It's a lesson we've never forgotten.

What she never had a chance to tell us were the lessons that society judges as proper things a woman should know — setting a formal table, sending thank-you notes for showers, putting out guest towels, giving a dinner party, the order in receiving lines. We had to learn those from other women. To this day we still believe that seeing a woman in the moon is a more valuable attribute.

Our father became father and mother during our rite of passage as young women in twentieth-century America. He quietly and capably helped with the cooking, shopped with us for clothes, and attended our "Mother-Daughter" dinners at the YWCA.

To cope with her grief, Lynn favored books — stacks of thick classics — that she devoured in the quiet of her side of the room. As a way to help Ruth vent her restless grief, Dad encouraged sports. He had always believed that girls should have more sports opportunities, that we could learn valuable life lessons from healthy competition, fighting on a field and forgetting it when the game ends. So deeply did he believe in our right to physical wins and losses, he organized girls' touch football games in the field behind our house. Ruth, who dropped the "y" in her name the year her mother died, quickly earned her way to quarterback.

We sisters were also learning about emotional endurance and about the power of the culture to shape and mold the way one behaves: "We don't talk about cancer," was a cultural rule we were reluctantly following. We were also learning about becoming independent women in an environment that was not yet ready for our independence: "Okay. Go long on this play. Hut-two, Hut-two, Hut-two. . ." We were a family of the nineties, thirty years too soon, and suddenly even more nontraditional in a very traditional town. With our same-sex role model gone, we began to realize that we would have to find our own way in a world that did not yet fully honor female explorers.

Everything had became so still at home after Mom died, and our return to school after her funeral was worse than being home. Our teachers would well up with tears just looking at us. Without mentioning it to each other, each of us sensed the need to get away from our grief-stricken town. It was as if the whole community had set an empty place for our mother at their tables. Within two years of our loss we both graduated from high school — Lynn, beautifully; Ruth, barely. We divided our clothes, curlers, and cosmetics and fled to colleges in different cities.

The nice thing about college was that nobody had mothers there. All of us were away from home and trying, for the first time, to think for ourselves. And male and female friendships were not based on neighborhoods or religions or a father's earning power. In college, not belonging was the good news.

We each had found a safe place to heal from the loss of our mother, to grow, and to figure it all out. It was like that space on our hopscotch board back home. Growing up we always played Snail Scotch on our little dead-end street. We chalked a shape like a huge Nautilus shell, a circle that got wider and wider as we went around from the center, and we marked it off into sections. Every time we made it all the way around the circle of steps, hopping on one foot, we could put our initials on one of the sections. Then, when we took another turn, the sections with our initials were our places to rest with both feet before continuing. College was a place where we each put our initials.

After college Lynn went to Alaska to educate children. There she earned her master's degree in education. From the ice-coated north, she next went to work in the open-air classrooms and tiny villages of East Africa. She had become a global woman by the time she married a fellow Peace Corps volunteer. At the time of her marriage in Africa, she was managing a sheltered workshop for people with leprosy in the central plateau of Ethiopia.

Lynn kept her maiden name and moved with her husband to an Indian reservation in New Mexico where she had her first son. She hyphenated her son's last name. She taught Native American kindergartners and flourished within a culture that sincerely valued women.

Ruth, much to her friends' surprise, traveled a traditional circle. After graduating from junior college, she leaped into love. She moved straight to a suburb only two hours away from their father. She gave up her maiden name for a husband who was going into his father's business. Within two years of marriage, she had her first son, a station wagon and a two-car garage.

When her second son was born with multiple handicaps, Ruth found herself thrust into a personal and political crusade to improve rights and conditions for disabled people. Along with baking cookies for the Scouts, she was now testifying at public hearings and picketing and protesting institutions that were mistreating disabled people of all ages. Within two years, Ruth adopted a Korean daughter and named her Bonnie Lynn, after her favorite childhood doll and her sister.

Though we lived in vastly different environments, our letters were filled with the similarities of our hopes, joys, and fears. We each wanted our young families to flourish in a safe and healthy world and we set about making those changes.

While Ruth was affecting change, one neighbor at a time, Lynn was a world away affecting cultures and traditions. While Lynn was establishing education programs for Native American children with birth defects, Ruth was teaching her own disabled child how to dial 911 on the telephone.

During the years that Lynn was learning Amharic to communicate with her Ethiopian co-workers, Ruth was learning sign language so she could speak to her son and his classmates. While Ruth was picketing a facility for the handicapped, Lynn was protesting radioactive pollution of Indian land in the Southwest.

We had honored each other's approach to marriage and, as time passed, we began to view the other's marriage as having the better chance of lasting. Sadly, each of our marriages began to disassemble, and we both eventually divorced. Like many women, we found that being a good wife did not guarantee a good marriage.

We had chosen to marry, we thought, to share our lives. Now we were tossed back into taking care of ourselves. Only this time with children. We poured out our pain of another major, crushing loss to the person who could best understand — a sister.

We had learned from Mom's death that life goes on and, so, with our constant flow of support through the mail, we each started back to school. Lynn earned a second master's degree - in public health. She later became a strong force in helping Ruth complete her bachelor's degree in journalism.

Only once since our high school graduations have we shared the same kitchen sink. For a glorious three-year reunion in the 1980s, we lived together as single moms with our assorted children. We had found another place on the Snail Scotch game to put our initials and, this time, it was the same space. After twenty years of hopping on our chalked sidewalk game, we found a safe place together and we rested and healed and tried to figure it all out . . . again.

We were so excited to be living together in the same house with our combined children that for weeks we just followed each other from room to room talking and hugging, laughing and crying, and speaking firsthand the poems of our lives.

We drove each other crazy. We drove each other sane.

Our children marveled at how much alike we were in so many ways. We parented the same way so our kids didn't have the opportunity to manipulate us as they had when we had lived with their respective fathers. Now the adults in the house were not fighting over the children. The sisters in the house were supporting each other.

We would often walk into the kitchen in the morning wearing the same colors. If not, we would be wearing each other's clothes. And our voices are so similar on the telephone that our friends, dates, and kids were often confused. We enjoyed stepping into each others lives through our voices and hearing directly the way people would respond to the other.

The kids would come up chattering behind us and be startled to discover that they were talking to their aunt instead of their mother and vice versa. They would say, "Aunt . . . Mom?" To this day we call each other Aunt Mom, and the kids still roll their eyes. And when we do have a rare opportunity to be close enough for us to touch and hug, we still show up wearing the same color. And our grown-up kids still roll their eyes.

We are again miles apart. Phone calls remain a luxury for us, but, in truth, we often prefer to write, brief or long, to share the triumphs and fears of now being middle-aged grandmothers in a culture that is still getting used to the songs we sing.

What would we have done without each other's caring packages of advice, mistakes, and examples? What does any woman do without a sister-friend to be her sounding board, her mirror, her echo, her pillow? As we struggled to either fight or welcome each stage of our lives, we reinforced our connection by sharing thousands of secrets with a million, trillion, zillion words.

Through the years we each developed into professional writers of newsletters, magazines, reviews, term papers, columns, poems, journals, books, proposals, policies, and devotionals. Our sister-missives, though, have always been the most fun to write, to ramble, to misspell, to rant, and to rhyme. Life is tough and we know it, but through our letters we have always keep our sisterness solid — sometimes funny, sometimes painful, always honest.

Although we have not been shoulder to shoulder for our rallies, protests, weddings, showers, and babies' births, we celebrate our love and support for each other through our words. The magic of these words continues today as we share the feelings of our far-reaching, worthwhile worlds.

I Miss My Sister!

She's a strong, determined woman
but not with me.

She's so fragile when we meet,
her eyes always searching
and vulnerable,
like a doe looking up while she eats.

My laughter frightens her.
Her face dissolves
like rain melting cotton candy.

I get excited when we're together
like a pet-shop puppy
licking, jumping, nipping at her.

I'm sorry she couldn't be here
for my crowded wedding
or when my babies burst in,
but that's different from missing her.

I miss my sister most when I'm alone
sewing
or curling my hair.

A Time to Love

A Time to Love

As young sisters living together, we didn't talk much about our very first crushes — the house was still too full of grief, but once we were away and trying out our new lives, the "love" letters started to flow.

Romantic love is something that girls grow up getting ready for. As we grew up, we were served myriad opportunities to learn, cafeteria-style, about crushes, flings, real romance, wrong romance, and true love. Only as we matured did we realize the magnificent, endless power of our love and our individual responsibility to understand, manage, and nurture the gift of love that all women possess.

Though living miles apart at a time when discovering and exploring romantic love was central in our lives, we sisters wrote to each other about the uneven, explosive power of falling in and out of and around love. We wrote through the learning curves of our boundaries, we marveled at our infinite supplies of different kinds of love, and we bemoaned our inability to yet honor all the dynamics of romantic love.

In the early years we often ended up crying and confused and writing it all out to our sister. As our lessons evolved from the first real kiss and first real romance to first lovemaking, we continued to share with each other the challenges of managing our innate and enormous flow of love. It seemed that we were always giving away huge chunks of ourselves, then painfully sweeping our fragments back, and soon looking for a new person with whom to create a safe place to let our love run free again.

We sisters, like every other woman in the world, were searching for someone to absolutely adore us, flip over us, and introduce us to parts of ourselves that we didn't know we had. Family loves us; that's a given. But whenever a new person, an outsider, loved us deeply, for even a short time, we knew we had been changed, and we needed to share that change with each other.

Our letters were also filled with stories of broken hearts, ours and theirs, as we made friends, made love, and learned a little more with each close encounter. Because monitoring our delirious, bottomless reserve of romance was such a huge responsibility, we continued to write about finding someone else who could help us use it, channel it, and receive it. We were expecting stability to come from our most volatile emotion.

In those brave young years, like most of the women of the sixties, we longed to attach physically and emotionally to a special man who would be able to hold our love, all our love. Love that ranged from the tenderness that made us cry when we were given a rose to the courageous force that stood up straight in the face of a trembling rage and declared, "I don't care how much you hurt me, I will always love you."

We read each other's descriptions of men we knew — men who we actually believed could return our powerful gift. We let them determine whether we were happy or sad, successful or useless, pretty or ugly. Since those years, we have often wondered how we would have behaved if we had been together then for shopping, movies, holidays, or even walks. Would we have needed so much from these unsuspecting young men? Would we have given less? Would we have taken less? Would we have learned our own value any sooner?

Only now, many letters and many years later, do we realize that the boys and men we knew back then were doing the same thing. They were learning the same lessons. They were equally surprised at their own responses, at the power of their own feelings. But males, we came to understand, don't seem to dwell on the same lessons that females do.

Women delight in the process of assaying what it all means; how it all feels, how it smells and sounds and tastes to know the full impact of our gift; to learn that love makes us feel the best and the worst we have ever felt. It is a wonderful, intriguing power to ponder. And, as sisters, we can and did relive it over and over. To understand the elevation and the impact of our own love is a powerful, pure joy. It's a joy to learn the contours of that mysterious land between men and women.

We also wrote clearly and loudly about our pain. We respected that special pain that deserved special attention. What better way to honor our pain than in our letters? Facing those feelings on paper was essential to helping us go on. When our hearts were full of broken glass, we smoothed the edges in a letter. When some man had disappointed us, again, we wrote each other all about it.

Many letters later, after our blistered hearts had scabbed and healed, only then could we begin to write about understanding that the boys and men of those days and nights just wanted the parts of themselves back. They wanted their secrets back, their exposed weaknesses covered up, and all the pieces back that they had given us in the hopes that we women could handle their love. They were experimenting with the most and the least of their love, too.

By writing those letters, we began to create our own definitions of love, definitions of what we wanted, what we expected, and what we would not sacrifice again just to feel the unrestrained power of our love. In the best of cases, our men grew with us. In the more emotionally expensive cases, we divorced and went on without them.

We still slip and slide backwards sometimes, but, with every living poem, we are learning the importance of trusting our boundaries and calling back our love when we have given too much away.

First Love

He smelled of English Leather
and wrestling mats,
my intense young man.

He wrote fragile poems
to rhyme my funny name
and drew pictures of me pouting.

He kept track of the times
we trembled in the back seat
safely hidden by damp
cloudy windows,
the car rocking our rhythm.

Young men now gallop by
with scrubbed faces
and feet that don't fit,
and I catch a whiff
of my first love.

That First Time

I can remember
when I thought
that love was merely moonlight
and flowers
and kisses
and that loving was for married people.

Then,
from the guiding of your hands and words
I learned love must be learned.
Love is trust and sacrifice
and the pulsing tenderness
of my flesh in crushing union with
the swollen focus of your love.

And depth of feeling vulnerable,
perhaps because we hide
no small thing of our deepest selves.

And strength of feeling, too, because
only love can make us
not mere single beings each alone.

And no more do I want to be alone from you.
To be alone is not to love.
And as much as I know how to love,
I love you.

Hands of an Artist

Light-headed, I arch
my back and groan
as you caress my spirit;
without touching my breast.

Valentine

It's his voice . . . and an old fairy tale
that lingers in the bottom of my heart,
in the folds of my sheets,
all tied up in my blue bandana.

I ache for his silk scarves and sweaty goblets,
and cashmere jacket, fluffy like a tan
teddy bear,
his raspy songs of longing and lust,
while his plants poured out of ceramic pots
like grey green fountains.
A real fantasy.

His name should have been Lance
but it was only George.
I wouldn't hear his real story.
I wanted only his romance,
his smooth, safe distractions.

Sayonara

I never said I'd love you FOREVER,
no, I'm sure I didn't.

I mean YES, we're COMMITTED and all
but I . . . well. It's really Peter Pan I love
for the way he rescued Wendy,
you know?

Don't you know how to play this game?

What do you mean it's not a game?

Sure it is.

I pretend to be weak and
you pretend to be strong.
But, really, I'm the strong one
and I'll be taking care of you.
Just like Wendy.

It has something to do with mothering.
Ask Freud or some of his friends,
or read Sayonara.
I cried reading it
because, you see, she'll love him forever.

Blueberries

Here I am on a Sunday morning.
Grey clouds . . . I hope it rains
to justify my staying in.
I have a date tonight.
My house is clean.
Situation stable. But oh,
I'd like to be in love today.
The other day I bought
a package of blueberries.
They tasted like dreamy days,
camping, hot sun
and being young.
For your birthday
I'm going to call you.

Romance

Lots of amber songs were sung
and toasts were made
beneath the patterned bars of shade
where,
fingertip intimate,
one of us said
"I love you."
Remember?
Of course
we do.

Double Jeopardy

A plain woman
turns beautiful and sad
from loving a loser
and losing her lover.

Adam's Rib

The story goes that Woman,
many virile years ago,
was given Adam's rib.

A calcium chunk
of male essence
to jump-start
our existence.

God, in her infinite humor,
gave us just a tiny token
of man.

And we have longed,
ever since, to surround
the rest of him.

And Adam?
All he really wants
is his own bone back.

Needy Moments

This dough resists me.
I kneaded it too much.
Isn't that what happens,
when you need too much?

If there's a place
that doesn't hurt,
I'll go there.

Being Single

It's funny about being single.
You walk around with
a machete in one hand
and a lasso in the other.

Men

They stay around long enough to
adjust the shower head.
I like this one's angle the best.

That's It!

These guys don't deserve
another breath of fresh air.
All my life, I've been giving them
CPR.

Valentines

Amazing what a Valentine
can do for a slushy week.
Most of my major mistakes
have come from not valuing
myself enough,
from trading myself for Valentines.
Valentines are just paper.
Self is all I'll ever really have.

Last Kiss

I didn't want the last kiss
to be his.
It's almost the only power we have.
I couldn't wear that kiss
all day,
no way.

Question

"Wouldn't you like to be in a marriage—?"
"No, I wouldn't like to be in a marriage—"
"Sorry, I was using the term restlessly!"

Mirror

He's a good mirror to look
into. I love my reflection
in his eyes.

Vows

Spurned
and turning off the light
on a fallen day,
we turn away
and spend the night
in icy non-recognition
of our promise
to love each other
even when
we disagree.

Crisp Toast

Eye to eye over biting it, we meet.
"Worried today, honey?"
"Yes . . . all that work . . . "
"Don't worry. You can do it.
How can I help you get going?"
"Make breakfast last a little longer."

Will You Be My Valentine

Will your touch make my heart turn over?
Will you hold me close when I'm scared and lonely?
Will you care when I get old and forgetful?
Will you be proud of my work?
Will you be patient when I'm trying something new?
Will you stop and pick up some tampons on your way home?

Partners

Several times
in the just right light
I found your face
older, frail, and like a mask.

I longed to reach
and touch the tired corner of your
mouth
and light your eyes.

What It's All About

Let's go to bed early
so we can snuggle-fasten ourselves
smack in a moist embrace
and sleep long peaceful hours
and wake up
all stretched out and feeling safe.

A Time
to Hope

A Time to Hope

With steady heartbeats and lifted chins, we sisters have always plunged into our recurring seasons of hope. These are fulfilling times for us. These are the times when we have been energized and focused and when our love is carefully funneled into a safe project, place, or person.

During this season, whether we are women creating babies, meals, office policy, legislation, or peace, the workings of our minds are introduced to the glories of our bodies and our productive potential is exercised. Whether we sisters were making a marriage, a family, a set of kitchen curtains, a quilt, or a better world, this gestating workout feeds our souls.

Some of us women may decide to "make" a book or "make" a business or "make" a research project into which we will breathe life. But for us sisters, our longest and strongest season of hope was the production and nurturing of our children. With the simple decision to become mothers, we began to write to each other about the intimate touch of a universal creative fertility.

Such a fertility handed us the chance to link with our female ancestors, to extend our genes, and to put ourselves into the middle of life's cycle. To be mothers as well as daughters. To sense hope for ourselves and others.

The season of hope wanes when the creation calls in its chips and demands we let our "babies" go. Although our offspring put us permanently in the cycle of life, we had to learn that each one has its own creative plan. Our creations are only visitors. We sisters still send encouraging words reminding each other neither to praise ourselves for their precious visit nor to blame ourselves for their departure.

It is hard to loosen the fingers that have held our own hands in place. But we remind each other that we must, so we can be free to create anew with each new season, new child, new partner, new project, new letter, and sometimes, new self.

The winds of creation are always in our letters, they whisper around us every time we rock a newborn baby — a tiny, tangible legacy of living. When we are rocking our creations, we are rocking ourselves. When we are writing to each other, we are writing to ourselves. When we are fueling our projects, we are feeding ourselves. We are filling up on hope.

Forceps Delivery

After months of you getting to be
a bigger and bigger butterfly
in my stomach,
we synchronized in a birth dance.
When long, shaking hours had gone by,
they reached for you with great tongs.

And out you slid,
long, strong, and balanced
like an airplane,
stretching the lengths
of your perfect limbs,
head turning,
eyes struggling open,
lungs filling with this new media, air,
yelling your surprise
to your father who was there.

Birthing

The swelling echo
of long, drawn life
forcing
head on bone, down and
up and out
and then the shout
of birth.

What else can a mother say
but "Yes, my lovely
baby!"
after what you go through
having them earthquake their way out
of you
the way they do?

When Billy Was Born

Blessings on you, labor-torn and squalling nephew
newly born.
Strong I pray your cells will be
from cyclamates and mercury
and presents of pollution we
who love you
have willed to you unwittingly.

And wait, there's more I wish for you.

May television not numb you,
may you learn to read easily
and learn other hard things the hard way.
May you never go to war,
may you love and be loved.

Wait, I've more,
you face-and-fist-and-wrinkled-knees
for as yet you have no name.

When you are grown and wish to blame us
for your cancered legacy,
be gentle.
We know our shame.

Celebration

Happy Mother's Day,
sister,
daughter of my heart,
for every baby cradled
and sweetly sleeping there
is one of us in song.

Folkdance

An infant
dances on his back
to the pulse of his own sob sounds.
Fists and feet in whirring dance,
he practices to run
   to climb
   to ride a bike
   to fight
   to build
   to fly
   to work
   to die,
all beneath the same
eternal sky.

Furry Mite

Playing
in a pretty suit,
hands on knees, smiling clear teeth
at a kitten
and saying "Deedledeele"
he named that cat.

And I'm hard pressed
to cold-shoulder that furry mite
purring in my sweet boy's arms
tonight.

Bonnie

Like a mother cat drawn to a sunspot on a windowsill
I am drawn to your light.
I want to stretch and yawn and purr in your warmth.
I want to rest in your sunshine.

Your screams will leave scars on my eardrums,
your growing means gray on my hair.

Yet, how soft and thoughtful you seem
when I kiss you asleep.

Sleep

When my baby sleeps
flung out on the mattress,
his grayish eyelids
deep in healing sleep,
I too want that cleansing, clearing
deeply breathed relief.

But that is not to be,
not tonight,
not for me.

Plotless dreams,
the images of night and day
pulling at me from far away
tangle me in a stringed net
near the surface.

Raising A Small Child
In A Small Trailer

It's hot
and our friends are far away,
so let's think of fish and reeds today
entwined beneath the linoleum
of our floating kitchen floor.

Our trailer sails
the summer air.
Horizons quiver over there
beyond the shining desert waves
lapping at the door.

We're on our way
to a sacred island in the sky.
To dig beside the turtles on the shore,
just you and I.

Writer and Child

The embryo sits in my lap as I type.
How does he know the right letters?
My child, he is three, glorious and free,
he knows the hymn of the poised type
klkkkjhaXXCZZZZXCVN
he releases a flow of ocean fish
upon the page.

A poem he writes with his pool-deep drum
on the dry trailer air
and listen there . . .
hear the future in his voice?

To Billy

I loved you, I nurtured you
I fought you, I hurt you

I suddenly felt grateful for all the moments
when I could touch your thoughts
and guilty
for all those times I lashed out at you.

You climbed those yellow stairs
with confidence
as if scaling a mountain
and I knew
you won't belong to me anymore.

Now I must share you
with your teachers
your peers
yourself.

Thank you, my son, for five swift years.
Courage . . . as we start our new careers.

Summer

Take a breath and relax the rules,
buy chlorine tablets for swimming pools,

late to bed on sticky nights
fishing trips,
mosquito bites,

hotdogs crispy from the grill,
popsicles and parks . . . until
the buses roll again.

Sweet September

We've memorized the bus routine,
dragged out the lunch boxes,
labeled the new clothes,
met the teachers.

Our summer days are distant smoke
as the autumn leaves are set on fire.

Hopes for the year are growth
for our children and ourselves.

The children learn to wave bye-bye.
We learn about new math.
They will learn to walk away.
We must learn to stay.

Parent's Resolutions I Will Try to Remember:

That a broken toy is as upsetting to my children
as a broken washing machine is to me.

That falling down a curb really hurts.

That being sick is sometimes scary
and always boring.

That saying "yes" and "no" means more
if I say "I love you" first.

That I'd be crabby, too, if all I could
see was people's knees.

That putting on your own hat
is as important as knowing your alphabet.

That discipline works better when they
need it instead of when I do. And . . .
that I can only work on all these things
one at a time.

Chet

Sure he's different from other kids
but that's no reason to give up on him.

Sure he can't talk
but don't be afraid of him, it's not
contagious.

We struggled with him to walk, to eat, to smile
but we didn't have to teach him to love.

He loves with no conditions
no loopholes
no restraints on his giving.

Most children are selfish,
so I guess he is different.
But that's not so bad.
He could have been born without the
ability to love.

Piranhas

One thing baby pets do for us
is keep alive that baby play idea
after our own kids have
turned into piranhas.

These Kids of Mine

I love them so, but yet,
I'm so pissed at them
I wrote a note
in all their lunch boxes,
In cursive.

Party, Party

I'm a Republican mother
and a Democratic lover.

Family

We're a tribe!
On one Christmas Eve
we filled one oaken pew
and shot the hymnal rapids
of a downtown, garnet church.

Candles gathered across the tall,
balsam darkness.
Inside, a grandson practiced being
born.

Outside, snow waited in a cold
silken night.
I suppose there was a sermon
but I didn't hear a word.

IQ

Motherhood knows
no IQ.

Happiness

You can't let your happiness
be determined by
your children's response to
you.

Sister, What Shall We Tell Them?

I never really knew her.
Our mother, I mean.
I never knew her as a person.
Just a Mother.

She died a long throbbing wordless dying.
Her eyes shut down on her secrets.
Before that she was our mother.

Sister, let's make sure
our children know us!

What shall we tell them?
Remember the night we drank gin
and laughed and cried
on the stairs
of the Bellrose Avenue house
and decided to be friends forever?

Or maybe dropping Dad's radio in the lake.
If nothing else, sister, let's tell them
we had fun raising them.

It will help them to know.

Leaves

When my children are grown and gone,
eating someplace else.
I'd like to take the extra leaves out of the table
but I can't.
They're cemented together
with pounds of spilled food . . . from laughing.

Grandpa

I watch you walking
down our friendly path,
the same steps we used to take:
today you're with my son.

You, man and boy who share
the same name, moving
together among the trees,
stalking squirrels and dinosaurs.

Your big hands hang easily
in sagging pockets, while your scion's
fists are crammed in his corduroys.

I am the link between my producer
and my production;
a gender apart.

Yet, I know what you're saying to my son.

A Time to Wish

A Time to Wish

This time began for us with our first deep breath of retrospection — like God's seventh day. It was like the day after the party when we ruminated on all our guests and all our hard work and we asked ourselves, "Did I have a good time?"

It was during the calm time after the newness of being brides and having a husband in our beds and our bodies. We each sat at our kitchen tables and looked at our slightly faded curtains or wash towels that matched or didn't match our once-new wallpaper . . . we picked up our pens and we began to wonder. And to wish.

Our children had long since taken their first steps away. They had spoken the first words they have to say . . . and we began to wonder. And to wish.

Our letters began to examine the whole picture that we each had painted, one energetic brush stroke at a time. Who really is this man I married? Has he changed since we merged our dreams and our income tax returns? Where is the romance I promised myself? Who are these children I have created and must let go? What were my dreams? Am I making them come true?

Through our letters, our wishes became real questions. A little voice from the child we were was saying to the woman we were becoming, "You're still young enough for somewhere over the rainbow, but this time write your own lines."

For us as maturing sisters, this was an especially difficult time. Once again we thought that we had carefully marked the spots on our Snail Scotch board, but the spaces we had created with such determination were no longer safe. Our correspondence increased as we each, separately and together, realized we needed to make new boards and create new spaces.

This time also meant the beginning of a deepened relationship with our female friends, our other sisters. Through these wishing years, we not only wrote about our haunting dreams, but we wrote to each other about other women we knew who were honestly sharing the beginnings of their own dreams, secrets, and fears.

A time to wish means there is still time! Things can still be different. But it's also a warning.

Just as we had learned about the responsibility of loving and creating, we began to realize that we can give our wishes no less respect. When our wishes come to visit, we must open the door and let them in, muddy shoes and all.

Chores

Burdens, heavy
like a storm-soaked coat,
I would shed if I could,
shake out,
hang up,
and sun dry.

Worries, binding
like pants too tight, too close,
I would pass on if I could
to stronger,
younger legs.

But chores,
the sorting, scrubbing, sanding
and soothing,
familiar and fitting
as an old bathrobe,
I would keep the same if I could.

Watch Out

The music and the supermarket smells
of celery and soup
follow me down the aisles.

Help!
I can't get away!
My cart is stuck!
Help!

Touch a purple cabbage and you're safe.
Hard to tell what's safe anymore.
Did you know they sell imitation milk?

Watch out they don't get you
in the supermarket.

Victim

Sometimes I feel like a fleeing zebra being
pursued
by my children and husband,
finally brought down by their varying needs.

Once gorged, they yawn . . . and saunter away.

Then come the domestic buzzards;
bills and repairs diving and ripping
at the horse-like carcass.
Blood trails the vultures as they plunge
into the defenseless, open rib cage.

The look of terror has left the striped beast's face
a blank-eyed haze.

My stripes show most at supper-time.

Stability

I want to reupholster my husband,
he's so settled into the armchair
of his attitudes.

Designer Life

Sometimes I feel like
General Mills designed my family,
Vincent Price designed my marriage,
and Marquis de Sade designed my bedroom.
Ya know what I mean?

Karen

Acquaintances, like chocolate mints,
are quick, tasty, and refreshing.
But to reach satiety
you need handsful.

You, dear friend, are chocolate mousse,
rich with lingering flavor
and rewards.

A little time with you
carries me a long, long way.

Patchwork Quilt

Sometimes, as I am scooting down the hall
to referee fighting children,
or rescue the cat from being stuffed into a doll's cradle,
I pause and catch a glimpse
of my patchwork quilt
frosting my bed like an immense
birthday cake.

My dessert is decorated with sprinkles
of ceremonial rituals and tender moments.
The golden ties stand proudly like candles
marking not chronological years,
but infinite motions of dedicated fingers.

In the time it takes to blink . . . I see
the remnants of my babies' christening gown
like soft, shiny dabs of white icing.

My first attempt at kitchen drapes,
like brightly colored nonpareils,
surprise the flowing fabric base.
The cloth scraps of showers and parties,
and P.T.A. dresses are bright confection squares.

Before I pick up the phone
or the broken toy
I stop and muse.
My patchwork birthday cake:
fabrics from social mile-markers
recycled to sweeten my memories
and keep me warm at night.

Joanne

Joanne is my friend because
she hears her own voice when I talk.
She listens. She nods. She smiles.
We cry together, too.
Our woman-selves reaching out
across the not-alikeness about us
to share the vibrations from
our woman-chores.
"My child . . . how best can I love him?"
"And about God . . . what do you think?"
"Is there one?"
"Years are passing. Are we growing?"

Erin

There's no one else
like you—and so
I'll always be a little lonely
for the gut-level laughing
we used to do
and long late talks
of finding out we shared
so many goblins
raging in our woman-selves,
and bringing out our dreams,
weak and wilted
from being hidden
from the assholes
who populate the world.

Sunday

Sunday, buffer to the cool week of current.
It used to be God's.
Now it's mine for good.
God's not really in church, you know.
She's home, playing with her babies
in a pie-fragrant house.

So Damn Mad

That's how mad you made me
by pretending you weren't mad.
Mad enough to
punch your shoulder,
walk away and
slam the door
shut
on you.
When you're mad at me —
say so.
So I can be mad back.

You Dumbhead

Round as a wedding ring
was your mouth
with surprise
when I said, "You've been with her."

You dumbhead,
don't you think I know you
right down to the sleep in your eyes?

Poetry For The Bathtub

Bubble bath in one hand
and faucets blended in a comfortable
song,
I slip into a medium
of soothing liquid
and add more hot.

Sinking back I let the hot water
sting me all over
until the boundaries of skin and bath
dissolve.

In the bath I wash away
everything that went wrong today,
and add more hot.

Pie Crust

On a snowy Sunday afternoon
I lay aside my wooden spoon
to take up a wine bottle, rinsed and smooth,
and set to rollingrollingrolling
the crust of a rashly promised pie
into the shape of Australia.

Why
are pie tins, dishpans, donuts, and brooms
records, rugs, and family rooms
cast in such careful monotony?

Weaving

Like a giant tapestry
guided by caring hands
daily in and out
slamming one year snugly
into the next with a shuttle.

Colors may vary,
the patterns may change,
but the texture of life
remains the same.

Purple Tablecloth

It makes me think of wine,
this purple tablecloth of mine,
and my passioned other self.

Is it the purple
making cool colors on my eyes?

Doubt

Sister, Sister.
Hear my prayer.
What is it, the strange fury that
makes me want to lash out at my child
and hurl my arms at people
and twitch
switch
see?
Don't let me forget
I have the strength to get
through this doubt
without
wounding
innocent
bystanders.

Until I Look Down

There is a restless boiling
under my breasts,
a surging through my arms and legs,
pulling me to the open window.

I am fleeing through the yard,
breathless at the edge of the woods.

I could spend days wandering
among the huge trees,
stroking their ragged trunks,
and sitting forever in the silent circus
inhaling the perfume of the earth.

Then I feel little vines wrapping
themselves around my legs,
tugging me back.

I look down and see my
children's bewildered faces
that need to be wiped, kissed, fed . . .

Mother Nature takes care of her children
and I will take care of mine.

A Time
to Cry

A Time to Cry

We embraced this time with full force, because it was such a relief. For us it heralded our internal permission to finally feel all the regret we had for all our disappointments and all our dreams that hadn't come true. That included all the mistakes, all the losses, all the things that weren't working . . . everything . . . all of it . . . right down to the last salty tear.

It took hard labor and many dark-inked letters to survive this time of honest insight. But our letters showed that enormous progress can be made in this raw time of walking about with deep puncture wounds on our dreams. We learned one new lesson in this time, too. Although our culture may expect our tears, society will recoil from our real, honest anger.

While the culture prefers ladylike depression, our letters were raw and honest. Sisterlike.

This cavernous rage is sacred for all women, as it was for us seething sisters. We put the cultural rules aside, knowing that it was time to honor the crippling terror we felt at having to carve out new lives — again. We'd followed most of the rules, and we were unhappy. We'd married whom the culture considered good men, and we felt trapped and controlled. We'd had great, exciting children, yet we still felt unfulfilled.

Our letters revealed that our lives had been defined by being someone's daughter, someone's wife, someone's mother. Now, for the first time in our lives, we were scared. We knew we had to take the risks that meant fighting for the spaces that our girlhood dreams had once filled — our dreams of an equal partnership with a man, our dreams of inner peace, our dreams of a space that we could fill on our own terms. We rejected being defined by whose report cards we were signing, whose laundry we were doing, and whose recipes we were preparing.

During this time to cry we often reminded each other that we already knew how to endure. This time it was the agony of finding out who we were as we stripped away each false face and dropped the shields of everyone else's coat of arms so that we could begin to create our own.

There is one small pleasure in this time. It signifies the very best time to be a victim because our culture understands, even supports, victims. Our culture says it's okay to play the victim when your life is falling apart. But we knew if we were to survive, really survive and heal, this time should be our last time to be a victim — the very last time that anyone could do anything to us again without our knowledge and our permission.

As we slowly went through the shock of dismantling our "we're-so-happy" lives so we could live honestly with ourselves, we needed to reach out to each other and ask our sister to celebrate our tears with us — for she truly has walked a mile in our high heels.

Not surprisingly, much of our writing during this time was filled with nature. We were remembering the safety of the forests of our childhood years before we had created our own households and our own families. We had long since rejected a formal spirituality which featured a punishing God. Now we began to reconnect with nature. We were feeling Mother Nature's rain in our hearts, her clouds in our thoughts, and we were building our confidence from her flowering forgiveness.

This time to cry is real. We earned it through our mistakes, from letting important feelings slip by without stopping and honoring them. We wrote once about a neighbor, saying, "She is so unhappy, she's got a terrific schedule." We knew from her story that if she weren't so busy, she'd be forced to feel her own regrets and rage.

We earned our crying time for all the times we hadn't listened to our hearts and we had pushed aside our own needs. We wrote of another neighbor, "Mrs. Kennedy comes out everyday and just stares at her unkempt garden. It's her patch of tears." Hers was the story of an overwhelmed woman who really longed to organize and nurture her own garden, but it would mean she would have to claim her own needs and that was too frightening for her.

And we earned our crying time by listening to a culture that decides a woman's worth by what she gives away and not by what she keeps and uses, like a family we once wrote of, "Very hard times — she's miserable, he's miserable, they have two beautiful children and every six months they have group pictures taken with fluffy pink clouds in the background. Do you suppose that is to keep them from crying?"

Yes, we earned a good cry and through our letters we used it wisely.

Storm Warnings

Brittle orange leaves rock and roll
in the cold wind.
Branches moan and wail
their winter warnings.
The air is wet and wild
but as yet — no tears.

A charcoal breeze twirls
inside my rib cage,
threatening a storm
building behind my eyes.
Restless and relentless
I search once more
for my foul weather gear.

Undertow

My fears, like a storm at sea,
surface, roll and spit,
then quickly sink beneath my smile.

Below the smooth skin veneer,
currents of pain pull and tug,
again to rise,

and vomit wet salty sorrow,
again to disappear beneath a shiny
crystal mask.

Yesterday's Brides

The organ pounds out its alert.
The parade begins with shiny, rustling cloth
as the spectators rise and turn
to watch life's virgins ascend.

The crowd is a field of garments and smiles
and married women softly crying.

The weeping wives are yesterday's brides,
with wrinkles around their dreams,
they watch their own ghosts pass;
cheeks blushed
with untarnished trust.

With the surging bar of music
that guides the bride's first step,
these matron tourists touch
their own memories ringing inside
before their hearts turn over
and go to sleep again.

Keeping Score

How long will we make each other pay this time?
We tally the debt
for years of coming home late,
for trips to the hospital alone,
for breaches of loyalty
drawn from a bank of memories
of when our love was new
and our scars came from the outside.

When was it we realized we couldn't
depend on each other?

When I go to weddings now,
I only watch the women in the pews
with bodies propped up by convention,
as the bride passes,
and inside, they're searching for the selves
they were —
before they started keeping score.

Pedestals and Vases

So what if he doesn't care.
I don't care either.
He stopped making me special.
I've got to be the only rose in the vase, you know.

So when he put this gladiola in next to me
I climbed down out of the vase and walked away,
thinking maybe vases isn't where it's at anyway.

Dear Lynn,

I buried my wedding rings today
in the bottom of my jewelry box,
under old charm bracelets and junk
that mean very little and very much.
I pushed my diamond into a velvet corner,
with unmated earrings and a lock of someone's hair,
against a yellowed scrap of paper
that I can no longer read,
but it smells like I kept it on purpose.

Dear Ruthy,

Dare to be alone.
Get drunk on solitude,
ironize your heart
to go on beating,
the sides of your mind to go on meeting.
Stretch slowly
painting an arc across the sky.
Breathe high
the tender freshness
of new life that says,
"I'm worth salvaging out of all of this."

Departure

Climbing away from the possessive planet:
a God's eye view of black greens,
blues, and squiggly tans.

The thick Ohio River, with its wiggling whiskers,
serpentines boldly
beneath me.

Crinkly hills textured with trees
are the fertile garbage left
by giant glaciers.

Clusters of shiny roofs and fibers of roads
 gather at the hips and knees
 of the mighty river.

Stick-size barges drift
from port to yawning
port.

Then the curtain of cumulus closes!
All I can see is
our severed selves.

Poplar

Holding the river bank at bay
with crumpled roots, like legs,
my ancient wooden Indian sits,
proudly watching as the water tumbles by.

His leafy headdress shades his baby shoots.
I crawl up in his lap to listen.
Against his ragged trunk I rest
as the river cries with me.

Refuge

Running
like a lost child
I sob my grief
to the open canyon arms
where I ask
the flowers
and blooming grasses
to let me in.

Clouds

Clouds in my head today.
Not the ones of cotton candy.
More like thick, cream soup;
my thoughts can't bubble through.

Send me a breeze
to blow away the blame.

San Diego Evenings

Night sounds shifting gears,
oil on the air,
street steps and a clearing throat.

Voices stretch up and down the street.
Somewhere a puppy yelps
and a back door swings shut.

Quiet as can be, compared to the daytime.
Ethiopian families are dying
one young son at a time.
We are the world?

This Time On Earth

The wheel
set us rolling away
from the timeless zone
and into now,
scaring the birds
and stirring the dust,
forming roads,
defining destinations,
goals, towns, maps,
rolling along
on fuels needled from the earth
and processed to fumes and heat
burping,
rolling, whining.

The processed sound of air
through engines,
harsh, hot, alive by force,
aimed at the ears of the sky
and piercing the membranes
just to say,
"WE DID THIS!"
AND THIS!
AND THIS!
HURRAH FOR US!"

Behold the fouled sky
and rejoice
if you can.

Rainset

Dark corners of sky,
clouds smeared earthward,
a symphony of sweeping rain.

I stand ankle deep in soaking grass
and wonder
if the daffodils are praying.

Flashback

I'm back in the Bristol Mountains — for a moment.
Billy is reaching over roots
to match steps with his father and me
who are, arm and arm, homesteading
the fluffy moss and ripe dank dirt.

"We'll build here!"
between the chilly streams that drip
down the mountain's wrinkles.
A little house for a little family.

Chester waits quietly in my womb,
not yet ready, to rip his way into our lives.

Rooting on the hillside, we, chins high,
own this valley . . . these trees.
The view is mine to breathe
and blow at my whim . . . for a moment.

Our lives will be smooth and safe, settled
on nature's ample brow.
We'll tip the rocks
and trim the trees and live.

And thin damp air will gallop into my lungs
filling them with tomorrow — for a moment.

Shoe Box

Our romance is in a shoe box
with wrinkled ribbons,
folded programs, cocktail napkins,
and kite string.

I see a four-leaf clover
you bent over
combing nature's carpet.
A Saturn-colored leaf we found,
the biggest on the street
when October started her
farewell fireworks.

I bury my nose in your letters
for a sweet scent from the past.
Memories are forever,
but the moments never last.

Beach Scene

Gulls walking foot-to-foot with their reflections
across the wave-washed patterned sands
turn to glance at me and stalk away.
"Humans, ah yes,
The ones who leave beer can droppings."
They seem to say.

The Doctor Said

The doctor said he looks angry and mad.
Well, now I can carry that around forever.
I'm not overly concerned.
I'll watch him closely,
ask him thousands of obvious questions
while peeling tomatoes or slicing peas.
I'll watch him sleep and hope
it is more peaceful than mine.
I'll plan special trips,
I'll be extra patient with his aching heart
and try to understand his crying
over me not having his favorite jeans
dry in time for school.
I'll do everything I can - except
go back with his father.

A Time to Cope

A Time to Cope

This is the time when we planted our seeds of sanity and hung on until we could see some signs of growth. Each day, each letter, we moved a little further from dramatics and a little closer to dignity. This was a thoughtful season for us. We were still sputtering, but our pain was less, our fears were quieter, our tears were smaller, and our hearts were larger.

With the rawness just behind us, we began to get promising snippets of what our futures could offer — new friends, new challenges, new energy. They were still just glimmers; our minds were still running the marathon that our feelings had just been through. Now was the time to rest our flesh and flex our thoughts, to stop rushing around and sit still and begin to learn to cope.

This was a dress rehearsal for becoming winners, for practicing how we wanted our lives to be and who we wanted to share them with. We began by re-examining our relationships and concentrating on our behavior, not theirs. We couldn't be with victims any more. We couldn't stay with men or women who were still feeding on grief. Our new roles meant new friends.

This new awareness began to spill over in how we related to our doctors, lawyers, teachers, and colleagues. Though still shrouded by the pain of the past, we began to reach our finger tips toward tomorrow. And often times we missed. New friends often carried old wounds and we realized that we must have, too, or we wouldn't have slipped back.

We wanted to speak with candor instead of whining or brewing and stewing like soup in a caldron. Yet, our voices seemed to crack like a young boy on the brink of manhood. We wrote to each other about how we wanted to feel and practiced what our new attitude would mean. We were safely being honest with each other. At the same time, we were rehearsing for the risk of honesty with our future friends and lovers.

This time was spent rehearsing being woman-winners in grown-up relationships by working on our own lines, not everybody else's. We were hanging on, taking two steps forward and one step back, and proud for our halting progress. When we realized that the people around us were not invested in our honesty, we tiptoed away. Not yet strong enough to stomp or swirl or fly out of their lives, we slipped away, and that was far better than slipping backwards. We were beginning to save ourselves unnecessary pain, and we were getting stronger.

During this time we worked on ourselves so that soon we could walk away, our backs straight, from a bad situation or too needy a person without blame, rejection, or a waste of time. On our good days, we could even envision ourselves not getting into that situation in the first place, but this all takes time and practice and retraining.

We sincerely missed our old worlds. For all the painful and stifling environments they were, the husbands, the neighbors, the former friends, they were still part of the life we once knew and once loved. They were relationships we had developed and lived with for most of our adult lives. And yet we had to leave them. And both of us agreed that we couldn't go back, not to those old friends, not to those old situations, those old expectations. Maybe never, but at least not until we were strong enough to maintain a new attitude with a new confidence.

It took a long time to secure this new attitude. Each day there was a bit more of trusting the way we felt as young girls and anchoring that trusting to the honest, happy women we wanted to become.

Through this time of coping we were finally together again, in the same house. This was a magnificent time for us. Sisters and children together and no husbands, we teased and hugged each other, we sang and failed, and we moved backward and forward together, slowly, cautiously, and honestly toward the selves we were determined to become.

Liberation

It's when you want to feel like a woman instead of a maid,
like a mother instead of a guard.

Many years ago you feathered your nest
decorated
dusted
baked
burped babies
and now it's your cage, your cell.

It's time to move on.

With warm woven memories and healing scars
you take that first feeble flight,
a little stronger, a little smarter,
and terrified.

My Sister Said

Hauling the dog house to
a new corner because
the dog was chewing
the cord that keeps
the pool alive,
my heart fell down
laughing when
my sister said,
"This wouldn't be
any fun at all
with a man."

Mother, May I?

Life is like playing Mother, May I.
Some get giant steps,
many sneak ahead when the leader isn't looking,
a few poor saps even get backward steps.

Me,
I just keep getting circle steps.

Everywoman

This life is a soap opera
a late movie
a sermon
a folk tale
a commercial.

Come and see it.
It's being filmed on location
at the kitchen sink.
You might even get a job
as an extra.

Angry

Angry
fur-spitting-tremble-voiced-mad
I am
whenever people crush me in a crowd,
another car blocks me in,
or dogs jump on me without hesitation!

Or
is it tremble-voiced-fear
I feel
and cannot forgive those who trespass
all over?

Prayer

I want to run outside
to rinse my hair in the singing wind
to swish my skirt
in crowds of grey-green sage
that feather the mountains' sandy scalp
and smell the vast old sting
of Earth
and pray away my rage.

Faithfully Questioning

Aching tooth,
Hell of a thing.
Must be God catching up with me for something.

The trouble with God-feedback is
it's so fragmented.
I've got no way of knowing for what.
Don't know which ways to mend.

Maybe I'm on the wrong channel
and Buddha is somewhere
smirking like hell at me and my aching tooth.

Single in the Burbs

What is it about evenings like this?
The air is clear and perfect,
families touching and talking
like a slow-motion movie,
voices drifting up and down the street
around manicured hedges and pines,
dinners spitting and smoking on backyard grills,
screen doors slamming.

What is tugging at my insides
when outside is so soft?
Why do I feel so far away
as the rusty sun moves closer
to the tree tops?

My legs are so heavy when the clouds
are so light. Yet . . .
I never feel restless in the rain,
only on lovely evenings when everyone
has someone to play with except me.

New Life

We went out a lot,
to the beach
and to friends.
Mentally, we were
kicking and scratching
at each other
and I was too tired.
Outside we were exhaling,
slowly, afterwards.
And then I would remember.
He's only (4), (5), (6) and
he's not my date. He's
the child, I'm the mother.
And next year he'll be only 7.
And I put him to bed
and go out with a man.
Or I go see a movie I can forget.

Flirting

Doesn't he know I have stretch marks?
Did he smile?
Doesn't he hear these kids calling me Mom?

He's walking this way!
Doesn't he know I sleep with my mouth open?
Can't he see my varicose veins?

There's a younger girl over there.
Does he see my fourteen gray hairs?

"Hi."

His voice sounds like a quick breeze
teasing the treetops.

I guess he knows but he doesn't care.

Riddle

What can you say to a man
who wants your body but
doesn't give a damn
about your hard-won self?

"What's in it for me?" you can say
to him.
Right into his arrogant face.
Look into his spoiled boy-child eyes and say,
"Yeah? What's in it for me?"

Try it, you'll like it.

The Play

I once loved a man
who would rather be
in hate with his ex-wife
than in love with me.

He decided this long ago,
years before I met him
in an upstate suburban bar.

This man wrote the play and
his ex-wife is the star.

I loved who I thought he was
sentimentally
from a distance.

There isn't any part I want
in that play.

Intimacy

Afraid I will want your touch
more than your laughter.
Afraid that I won't.
Afraid we can kidnap only
one moment.
Afraid we won't.

Afraid once I stand naked
before you,
you'll no longer see my clothes.
Afraid once we cross the boundaries
of skin,
mental foreplay will be numb.

Afraid once we explode and shiver
in each others' arms,
I will awake to find only your prints
on my pillow.

The Morning After

When we have touched
and groaned
and I come home
with the smell of you
on my clothes,
I dream of touching
evenmore,
evermore.

But his eyes . . .

Even as we danced on bride-white beaches,
I wondered how the end would feel.
The waves left souvenirs of sand
in the hems of our pretty clothes.
We were swallowed by the bright black sky.

It was easy to trust his words.
You see, my ears are without suspicion.
But his eyes? Just rarely, his eyes would fill
with terror or madness and then blink
back to soft opals of blue.

His arms were strong and sure of themselves,
his body a comfortable place for tickling,
telling and loving.
His laughter left me loose.
But his eyes . . .

I Hate Goodbyes

I weed the garden and see your face,
rake the leaves and feel your breath,
read the Sunday paper with your name
in my mouth.
My fingers dial your number
on the table, in my pocket, but never touch the phone.
I hardly remember the words we spoke,
my ego was screaming so loudly.
I replay it in my mind almost forever.

You resurrected parts of me
I thought were surely dead.
I watched our touching from a distance,
drifting, hearing things I've never said,
passion rushing to the surface of my skin,
weeping with a warm heart as we danced
in our love freely, safely, together.

I will always love you
and when the throbbing stops
we should be friends.

Wind

Wind, blow through my soul
and take the tangled webs
of detailed fear I feel
and scatter them behind me
on the ground
to dissolve
and disappear.

Dry and cool me
like the leaf-tossed branches
of green on green
against blue grey sky.

Sing air sounds around me.
Rub my face with gusted fingertips,
hold my clothes to me,
make me whole.

Lessons

"I can't, I can't, I can't,"
I say
until I must.
A new friend said,
"Hitch up your girdle and
go another mile."
And so I plow through some
deep, tangled task
sometimes
coming to an end
of light,
holding
happily
in my hands
some answers
and tools to do
what's right.

New to the Business World

Swamped, still standing
in a coil of dread,
I ask your name
and letterhead.

Needlework

I splash out green satin
on the kitchen floor.
My mind flows on, cutting
the shape of my three favorite dresses at once
plus the tea-glass lines I used to be
plus sagging lines
for humility.

Play down the breasts.
Needs a good solid belt.

There, whoever you are, my changing self,
plunging along in life,
you're dressed.

Fear

The old fear is seeping back,
crawling overhand up my ribs,
pounding in my ears.
Please, sister,
give me some of your strength
to bring home, to carry in my yawning arms
and press against my shaking self.
Lend me some of your power to squeeze in my fists
until I am safe again.

A Time
to Heal

A Time to Heal

This was the springtime of our evolution. Still together in the same safe house, we gradually began to notice the absence of our pain. We began to feel lighter, younger, and warmer, like a spring day.

Side by side, we began to take off our emotional mittens and muffs and feel the air around us. Life is not without its surprises and disappointments, but once we began to heal, we knew deep in our bones that we would never again be as afraid or as lonely as we had been.

Healing means forgiveness and forgiveness takes time. Yet, one day, we each separately bumped into our old pain and discovered it didn't hurt anymore. We rejoiced at realizing that our past hurt couldn't send the same cold chill through our bodies, that it couldn't make us curl our shoulders to hide our slamming heartbeats anymore.

Instead, we could calmly recall, "Ah, yes, I remember this, this is old pain, but I don't feel its sharp edges anymore." And we moved on. Just as every springtime will forever forgive the icy fingers of winter, we began to forgive ourselves for whatever we thought we did wrong.

Then, very slowly, we began to forgive our wrongdoers because we had learned that abuse can't happen to us anymore. From where we stood, together, in the sunshine and warmth of our evolving confidence, we were even prepared to forgive future wrongdoers — the ones we hadn't yet encountered and who might set out to break our hearts, take our jobs, or frighten us away from life's feasts.

It was finally in our power to experience and practice a happy present and a hopeful future, to experience a creative lifestyle and to try some new choices. We held hands and jumped into our newly healed lives.

The little mementos of misery we each had kept could now be gently shelved. It was time now to create our own diplomas, our certificates of good health in recognition of fulfilling all the requirements of being well.

The circle was complete, and we knew what was next. It was time to separate again, to breathe and bloom apart like so many years before. We stood together over a second fresh grave. The grave of our pain and grief. We again divided up our clothing and curlers, hugged each other, and said goodbye, this time to the women we had become and the niece and nephews we had shared.

Ruth packed up her computer and her clothes and turned her car south to start a new life as a writer in a beach community of strangers, full of sunstruck tourists and established locals. Lynn headed a short distance west to a career in public health in a rural county. This time she was the one who chose a place that was close to Dad.

We knew it was time to test our state of health — alone. We knew we were not running away. Instead we were running toward our new lives. We knew it was time to write again our letters to each other instead of to speak them. We knew it was our springtime from the sound of our own, forgiving laughter.

Healing

From grief to relief:
I feel like a chameleon
walking over the funny papers.

Renewal

Love, like a bamboo stalk,
is strong;
smooth,
the color of sun;
with scars from seasons of growing,
deep cracks leaking unfinished feelings,
brittle from betrayal.
Yet, in time, strong again
and shining, carrying the stress of the days,
bending,
and vaulting us on.

Spring Cleaning

It's time to clean out the shelves
in my mind's attic,
pull out boxes of guilt, confessions;
decide to set some free,
refinish special memories,
restore musty ideas that are back in style.

Some thoughts go to the goodwill box,
on to other mothers, other families.
A little piece of pain goes dusted
back on the shelves
(I can't let it all go at once).
Some laughter still fits.
The rest of the treasures go into my letters,
to make room in my attic—

for new smiles,
new secrets,
new stories.

New Life, New House

Indeed, you are an indulging little shelter,
my little old, new house,
all shrunken and shriveled,
as if washed in hot water, and then sun dried.

Your puffy curtains, too full for the windows,
compete for space in the rumpled rooms
as sand scratches at your door like a hungry kitten.

Ancient dunes and sea oats salute your porch
and yard, where the mighty Atlantic
softens into the forgiving bay.

Your sidewalk is cluttered with meniscus jellyfish,
like ice cubes reluctant to melt.

Above your wrinkled roof, indignant gulls screech
of supper time as God's pink gaslight touches the sky,
and I softly cry,
for I am home at last.

Virgin's Island

Butterfly sails snap and sway
where water meets the hot wind,
as the ocean, aqua and teal,
teases whitewashed sand.

Mountains burst from the sea,
spiney backboned, ragged and old,
as waves spit at the rusty rocks
and the tide turns shells to sugar.

The beach is a gracious graveyard
of ancient boulders and innocent coral,
skeletons and scraps worn smooth
from a salty tongue.

Each day another barnacle
leaves my weary hull
and floats away.

The conflict here is with the sea;
not me.
I watch her roll and curl,
grind and play.

My battles are but a splash
in the vastness.
Her fury calms my own.

The Goddess Within

She blows through our lives
like a storm at sea,
heaving, curling,
slapping our breakwall
with waves of self-awareness.

She recedes like the tide
leaving us stranded on sand,
exposing bony spikes of strength.

Only those brave enough know
the turbulence begins
as a single salty tear.

Sundays

Stagnant odor of steel and flowers,
notes from pious, black robed towers
reach across rainbowed glass.

Seats bound loosely, rigid rows,
creaking, moaning mellow and low.
How many years have passed
since my smaller, softer, shinier shoes,
ruffles, ribbons, pinks, blues?

Familiar boards sigh when trespassed upon.
My light step is gone.

I carry my share of blessings and blame,
loving, lying, friendship, and pain.

I'm Not Musical, Though

My dad
he sings and sings,
for the hell of it,
for the joy of it.

It's from him I learned to sing,
just to open up and aim,
swell with the song,
taste the words,
warble those favorite phrases,
soak your throat in long, loose bottom chords,
sing out the story notes,
and give the chorus all you've got.

Sisters and Mothers

Sisters and mothers,
are we not from the same moon?
A together-dance ripples up through our ankles;
seasons call to us from within.

Link arms with arms and turn a slow south turn
of strainless prayer.
Pull your arms up overhead: untie your hair.
Stretch on strong legs,
touch the clouds.

Earth lives in us.
Let the scented winds rejoice around our bare arms.
Dance together, daughters,
galaxies apart.

Wellness

To emerge strong
from a man's bed
is one thing.
To emerge strong
from my own
is another.

Crocus

Proudly peeking through the snow,
somehow they always seem to know
it's time to live again.

Pushing up to find their places,
tulip red and velvet faces
waiting for the rain.

Windows open everywhere
welcome sweet and sunny air.

How can we complain?

The Sister Genre

We decorate the same, you know
with our braided rugs and calicos,
our plants and prisms in the windows
tossing splotches of color against the walls.

We save the same slivers of soap,
slips of paper, plastic lids, and bread ties,
but never enough safety pins.

I can visit wherever you are,
and find my own kitchen smells,
and children playing on the moguled floor
with spools and pots and pans.

Our glitzy beads have always hung
beside our toothbrush and tweezers.
We still overcook red meat,
and wonder why men are so . . .
whatever.

Do you suppose it's all genetic?

You

play me like a finely tuned instrument,
strumming, striking my inner chords,
notes I've never felt,

skillfully breathing my rhyming passion,
a symphony I've never heard,
a song I've never sung.

A Time
to Begin

It's Time

It's time to write again, I feel the pulling,
pacing in my heart.
A poem is brewing in my creative crockpot,
words simmering, bubbling.
But what to write: the March on Washington?
My summer vacation?
My unknown uncle, now dead
from well-known causes?
My daughter's wedding?

I want to write about a woman
who is sick of sweeping dusty dreams in a circle.
She's grown, she's loved, she's fought,
she's pleased.
She's walked the floors with a crying,
dying child.
She's seen it all, she knows it all.
Now she's ready
to begin again.

Epilogue

Epilogue

Like women, this book has been through many changes. Over the years, we have taken turns arranging and rearranging our collection of letters like flowers in a vase. Each turn we took was an intimate gift to the other as encouragement to become more secure, more confident, and more complete.

From this printed perspective we ourselves are surprised at some of our life's choices and struck by how far we've come. Yet, we can clearly see what we have always felt: that women, especially sisters, profoundly affect each other's lives whether we are sharing a house or sharing the world.

As sisters we teased each other about whom Mom and Dad liked best, about which aunt or uncle liked which one of us best, about who had better hair or thinner legs or who was smarter. With this collected correspondence in hand, there is none of that competitive chatter.

We don't remember which one of us wrote which lines unless there is mention of a special name or location. Ownership has never really been important to us because these passages of time and rites and prose belong to every woman.

Our rare moments of conflict are absent from this book because our conflicts meant and still mean the absence of letters. Such silence leaves us each feeling alone and out of sync. We wait out those scary moments until they have been diluted by passing days. Until they can be gently touched and talked about. We know our bond is forever. We have the time.

We've never challenged each other about how we parent or who we choose to sleep with or how we cook. We don't have that right. Our conflicts come from not understanding what the other one needs from us at a particular time — sympathy, empathy, encouragement, or simply an ear.

Through the years, whether in calm or after conflict, we have always written about making choices to better our lives, our situations, and our families. Choices to best maintain our sense of worth and our sense of joy.

Our decisions have resulted in the creation of five amazing and diverse children. Through it all we have survived hirings, firings, college degree programs, great loves, divorce hearings, custody battles, marches, surgeries, holidays, and rejection slips.

And now, one sister with a new husband and the other sister with a new career, we intend to embrace an exciting new project together with the same curiosity and courage — our middle age.

We live several states apart once more and our future letters, no doubt, will be filled with the dreams and choices we will have for the rest of our lives. We're even considering getting matching tatoos in a place where they won't show.

We've already started teasing each other about being doting grandmothers. We imagine ourselves becoming wise crones to the next generation. We sincerely welcome our time of passing the torch to them, our daughters and our granddaughters and the next wave of sisters.

They are so strong, these women of tomorrow, and so sure. They will call upon their sisters, younger and older, to guide them along this wonderful, intriguing journey. They will succeed and sometimes fail with honor. They will love men and women and leave them and love again.

Their sisters among them will be lawyers, doctors, pilots, homemakers, single and married moms, astronauts, athletes, and leaders. And they will know success and independence are the natural order of life. They don't need to be reminded of how it used to be. They can feel that ancient struggle deep inside. They will keep the momentum going.

That is certain.

What Color is Your Doctor?

Now that I am a grandmother,
I feel blessed if my doctor is a woman.
But short of that, I'm happiest if my doctor is
black, or tan, or olive, or yellow, or red.

Because I know that in their hearts,
in their colorful heritages,
in their diverse DNA
in their bones,
they respect me
because my hair is gray.

I may not understand their lyrical accents,
(my white pharmacist can translate)
but in my ethnic doctor's eyes and touch
I can trust their ancient cultural code
to revere me because I'm old.

Our Special Place

Flee
to the flea market.
Stroll the long aisles
of sorted piles
of bright old things
with a slow wane of care.

And from the distant depth
of wherever you are,
I'll meet you there.

Memories of My Sister

I like wearing your old gloves –
it feels like you're holding my hands.